Job
Smarts

Lucy O'Neill

Children's Press®
A Division of Scholastic Inc.
New York / Toronto / London / Auckland / Sydney
Mexico City / New Delhi / Hong Kong
Danbury, Connecticut

Book Design: Michael DeLisio
Contributing Editor: Jennifer Silate
Photo Credits: All photos by Maura B. McConnell

Library of Congress Cataloging-in-Publication Data

O'Neill, Lucy.
    Job smarts / Lucy O'Neill.
        p. cm. — (Smarts)
    Summary: A guide to determining one's own skills and career goals,
    finding helpful resources, writing a cover letter and resume, and
    interviewing for what could be—or lead to—a dream job.
    Includes bibliographical references and index.
    ISBN 0-516-23928-7 (lib. bdg.) — ISBN 0-516-24013-7 (pbk.)
    1. Job hunting—Juvenile literature. 2. Vocational guidance—Juvenile
    literature. [1. Job hunting. 2. Vocational guidance.] I. Title. II. Series.

HF5382.7 .O54 2002
650.14—dc21

                                                                    2002001906

Contents

Help Wanted:

Summer internship available. Small company in search of intelligent self-starter to work in a fast-paced office.

What is your dream job? What kind of job would give you a chance to use your skills, be challenged, and have fun? It is never too early to start thinking about your future career. You can start learning the skills you need to get your dream job now. In this book, you'll learn how to write a great resumé and cover letter. You'll also learn how to have a successful interview. With time and practice, you'll be on your way to landing the job of your dreams.

Take a look at the classified ads in your local paper. Your dream job may be waiting.

FULL-TI

Ready, Set... Plan!

If you are a student, finding and keeping a job can be tough. Your schedule is already full of classes and homework. You may be worried that having a job will add more stress to your busy life. Even a summer job can mean less time for playing sports, traveling with your family, or hanging out with your friends. You can find a balance that works for you. All you need is a good plan.

You Have the Skills

The first step in getting a job is to get to know yourself. Schedule some time when you won't be interrupted. Try to avoid distractions like television or loud music. Use a notebook, journal, or your computer to write down your thoughts.

It can be difficult to juggle school work, sports activities, and a part-time job. Make sure your schedule works for you.

First, think about your skills. Make two columns for your skills. The first column should be job-related skills. What computer programs do you know? How fast can you type? Can you file? Can you use a cash register? All of these are job-related skills.

In the next column, write down skills that aren't job-related. These skills are called "transferable skills." They are skills that can be transferred from your life to your job. Don't worry if your answers don't seem connected to a job search. You might write: I'm a great guitar player. A guitar player might enjoy working at a music store or interning with a small orchestra. Someone else might write: I'm good at math. Maybe there's a local accountant who needs seasonal help. There are no right or wrong answers when you're listing your skills.

The process of making this list will help you in several ways. First, it will help you when you write your resumé (we'll get to that later). Writing a list of your skills may also help you think of job possibilities that hadn't occurred to you before. If you have a hard time coming up with a list, ask your friends or family

members to help you. Sometimes, other people will see things about you that you don't see in yourself. Your list could become much longer than you expected.

Here is an example of a skill list:

Job-Related Skills	Transferable Skills
Type 30 words per minute	Can play guitar well
Know MS Word and WordPerfect	Like to read
	Good with kids
Can file	Good at math
Can use the Internet	Like to draw
	Good organizer
	Good writer

Part of looking for a job is to decide what you want from it. Write down the reasons that you want to get a job. Do you want extra money to buy CDs or clothes? Maybe you need money to help pay for

college tuition. Maybe you want to get work experience. These are all good reasons for getting a job.

Full-time or Part-time?

Now that you've listed your skills, think about how much time you have for a job, school, and other activities. You need to know how much time you can work each week before you start looking for a job. Use a calendar to see how your schedule looks. Be sure to allow enough time for homework and any other things that you may have to do.

If you are a full-time student, then you are only available to work part-time during the school year.

Heads Up

Don't limit yourself to retail jobs at the mall or food service. If you have a business idea, why not think about starting your own company? K-K Gregory was ten years old when she created Wristies, a fleece sleeve that covers the gap between a coat and a glove in cold weather. At seventeen, Derek Ratke was running his own woodworking business. If you're careful to get help from professionals when setting up your company, you're only limited by your imagination!

Even your favorite hobbies might lead you to the job of your dreams.

11

If you are hoping to earn enough money to buy a new car, then working part-time at the mall might not be the best choice. You probably won't earn enough money to reach your goal. Working full-time as a lifeguard in the summer might be a better option. Being honest about your schedule and your goals will make your job search easier.

Networking

Now you have a list of things you are good at and a list of goals you want to reach. You also know how much time you can work. Now, try to think of ways that you can combine all three things.

Imagine jobs that could put your skills to use. If you are a very organized person, you could use your organizational skills at jobs in many different kinds of places: offices, banks, or libraries, for instance. If you like to cook, you could work in a restaurant, bakery, or coffee shop. If you paint or draw you could work for local newspapers or design posters for theater groups, for example.

You can get valuable career advice by talking to a professional. You might even be able to find a great job or internship in the process!

Each person will have different work ideas based on his or her skills, goals, and schedule. If the lists you made don't make you think of a particular job, talk about your search with family and friends. They may know of jobs you hadn't considered.

Talking with other people about your job search is called "networking." By talking with others, you are building a network of people who might help you in your search for work.

One great way to network is to interview some-one who is working in a field that interests you. If you like animals, you could speak to a veterinarian or a zookeeper. By speaking to someone who is already a professional, you can learn how he or she got involved in the field. They may be able to give you advice about finding work that would help you reach your goals.

Where Do I Look?

There are many resources available that can help you find a job. One source is your local newspaper. The "Employment" or "Help Wanted" section of a newspaper has dozens of listings from different employers who are looking to hire the right people. These listings will usually give a brief description of the job opening and the phone number or address of the company that is offering the job.

If you have access to the Internet, you can visit a job search site. Many of these sites, like *snagajob.com* and *summerjobs.com,* have great information for your job search. You can usually fill out applications or post your resume on these sites, allowing employers to look at them and contact you if they want.

You may also want to call local businesses to find out if they are hiring. Introduce yourself to whomever answers the phone and ask to speak with the person who is in charge of hiring. Tell that person that you are interested in getting a job with the company. Ask him or her if you could set up a meeting to tell them about yourself and learn about possible job opportunities.

School is also a good resource when looking for work. Guidance counselors often have a lot of job information. Find out if your school has job or career fairs, where employers set up information booths about jobs they are looking to fill. Your teacher or school librarian may also know of places to look for a job. They may also have names of employers who have hired students in the past.

Chapter 2

Cover Letters and Resumés

If you stick to it, your job search may soon pay off: you find a company where you want to work and the company is hiring. Now what? Some companies just ask that you fill out an application. However, many companies ask for a resumé. A resumé is a document that gives future employers an idea of who you are, what you're good at, and what you're hoping to get out of a new job. A good resumé will help you land a great job.

Your Resumé

Writing a resumé doesn't have to be scary. In fact, it can be a good way to learn more about yourself.

Sending out more than one resumé at a time can increase your chances of getting an interview.

The lists of skills and goals you created will help you write a strong resumé. Having a good resumé shows a potential employer that you are focused and aware of your own abilities. It also shows off your communication skills. Even if you don't need a resumé for the job you want, most employers will be impressed that you prepared one.

The purpose of a resumé is to share basic information with employers. The resumé should be brief and clearly written. The main parts of a good resumé are:

1. **Contact Information** (your name, address, phone number, and email address)
2. **Objective** (a short description of what you are seeking in a job)
3. **Work Experience** (if you have any—don't forget volunteer work and baby-sitting!)
4. **Education** (describing any classes that might be relevant to a specific job)
5. **Special Skills** (things you can do that might be important to the job, such as computer programs or foreign languages)

Writing a rough draft of your resumé will help you to organize what you want to say about yourself.

Be sure to check your spelling when you have finished typing your resumé.
Most computers have a spell-check program that can help you find mistakes.
A resume that has errors may stand in the way between you and an interview.

Take a look at Alicia's resumé. Alicia is looking for a summer job to help pay her expenses when she goes to Brown University in the fall. At Brown, she plans to major in finance. She is sending her resumé to local banks and accountants.

Alicia Morrison
1234 Brighton Drive
Helena, MT 59601
(406) 555-6789
alicia@morris.net

Objective: I hope to use my organizational skills in a summer job with a focus on finance or accounting.

Work Experience:

January - March 2003 **Walk for the Cure Marathon**
Coordinated the collection of pledges for local chapter.

Summer 2002 **Java Joe's, Helena, MT**
Provided customer service in a fast-paced environment. Operated cash register and espresso machines and organized inventory.

Education:

1999-2003 West High School, Helena, MT

2003 Organized a plan to upgrade hardware in the computer lab.
2002 Served as Treasurer of the Junior Finance Club.
2001 Represented sophomore class on the Student Council.

1997-1999 Lester Junior High School, Boulder, CO

Special Skills:
Computer programs: MS Excel, Adobe Photoshop, MS Access, Quicken

A neat, carefully thought-out resumé will impress potential employers and help your chances in your job search.

Alicia doesn't have much experience at paid jobs, so she focuses attention on her school activities and volunteer work. Her resumé shows that she has handled finances for student organizations. It also shows that she has worked with charities and has organized different kinds of projects. Her work with the student council also shows that she has good leadership skills.

A resumé doesn't need to give all the details of every job or project. It just needs to catch the eye of an employer so that he or she will call you for an interview. Alicia can talk about the details of her resumé during the interview.

Action Words

When writing a resumé, it's important to use "action words." Look at Alicia's resumé. She uses the words "coordinated," "organized," and "represented" to describe the things she has done.

Heads Up

Be sure that your resumé and cover letter are printed on nice paper and that the ink is dark and easy to read. If your printer is running out of ink, or if you don't have a computer, most copy centers have computers and printers that you can rent. This simple step will make a great first impression.

Have someone else read your resumé. They may have helpful suggestions and find errors that you didn't see.

These words are more powerful than just saying "I was the treasurer," or "I was in charge of helping volunteers get pledges."

Action words make it possible to describe something in a shorter way. Since a resumé is designed to provide a lot of information in a small amount of space, using action words is important. On the next page is a list of action words you can use. There are many others you will think of as you begin writing your own resumé.

arranged	explored	prepared
built	handled	reviewed
contacted	invented	sold
created	managed	tested
developed	operated	trained
directed	planned	wrote

Resumés come in many styles and sizes, but they should all be neatly typed and grammatically correct. If you have any doubts about the language or spelling of your resumé, you should have someone check it for errors. A resumé is meant to show the very best things about you. You don't want to give a bad impression with spelling errors or poor typing.

Cover Letters

Your resumé is finished, but your work isn't over yet. You still need to write a cover letter. A cover letter introduces you to an employer. You should use a cover letter to tell the employer why you're the right person for the job. A cover letter is usually sent or given to a potential employer with your resumé. There are a few simple rules to follow when writing a cover letter:

1. **Keep it short.** A cover letter shouldn't be longer than one page.
2. **Be confident.** Even if you don't have a lot of experience, your willingness to learn is a big plus!
3. **Use action words like those in your resumé.**
4. **Proofread!** Nothing turns off an employer more than spelling and grammar mistakes.

When writing your cover letter, mention the skills that you can offer the company. Be sure to address the letter to the person who is hiring. Finally, put your contact information on the cover letter as you did on your resumé. Here is a sample cover letter that may give you some ideas:

Alicia Morrison
1234 Brighton Drive
Helena, MT 59601
(406) 555-6789

December 7, 2003

Mrs. Fran S. Freedman
Accounts R Us
400 Money Road
Helena, MT 59601

Dear Mrs. Freedman,

I am writing in response to the advertisement in the *Helena Herald* for a summer position with your firm. I believe that I may be the "intelligent self-starter" that you are looking for.

Throughout high school, my studies and extracurricular activities have helped me develop my organizational skills and mathematical ability. I've taken a leadership role in school and in my community, volunteering for a variety of causes while maintaining a 3.2 grade point average. I am starting at Brown University in the fall, where I plan to pursue my interest in finance.

I will phone you during the week of December 12 to discuss the position further. I look forward to speaking with you.

Thank you,

Alicia Morrison

Chapter 3

Interview for Success

It's an exciting moment when you get a call from an employer to come in for a job interview! The interview is your best chance to get the job. It pays to be prepared. The interview is your chance to make a great impression. Here are a few tips to help you get ready:

1. **Be prepared.** Learn as much as you can about the company. Check out their Web site, if they have one, and talk to friends who may be familiar with the company. This way, you can ask great questions during the interview. Before the interview, brainstorm questions that you might like to ask. Also, be sure to bring along fresh copies of your resumé. The person interviewing you may want a copy.

Make sure you write down the date, time, and place of your interview. If you miss the interview, you may also miss out on the job.

2. **Be on time.** To be safe, be early! It's also a good idea to call the day before your interview to confirm the place and time of your appointment. Ask the interviewer if there is anything that he or she would like you to bring to the interview.

3. **Be clean and well-groomed.**

4. **Dress appropriately.** It's better to be too conservative than too casual. You will look more professional, too. Also, don't bring things like cell phones or beepers that may interrupt the interview.

5. **Be confident.** Look your interviewer right in the eye and feel confident about your ability to do a good job!

Alicia's Interview

After sending her resumé out to local financial businesses, Alicia was asked to come in to interview with a small accounting firm. She described the experience of her interview:

Looking and feeling your best will create a great first impression.

"I was excited that Mrs. Freedman called me for a job interview with her accounting firm. I had mailed her my resumé and cover letter in early December. After checking my schedule, I set up an interview with her on a Wednesday afternoon at 4:00 P.M. I would finish my last class at 2:00 P.M., and still have time to go home, change, and get ready.

I called on Tuesday to confirm my appointment. Mrs. Freedman's secretary told me that the office had a casual dress policy. I decided it was better to be safe. I wore a black skirt and blazer with a white blouse.

The office was a 20-minute drive from my house, so I left at 3:15 P.M. I pulled into the parking lot at about 3:40 P.M. I sat in the car for a little while, concentrating on the reasons I felt that I should be hired for the position. I checked in at the receptionist's desk 10 minutes before the appointment and she asked me to take a seat. Just as I sat down, my cell phone started ringing. I was so embarrassed. I quickly turned it off. Luckily, Mrs. Freedman hadn't come for me yet. When I looked in my bag, I realized that I had forgotten extra copies of my resumé. Now, I was incredibly nervous.

Confidence is the key to having a successful interview. A firm handshake can make a difference.

Before I knew it, I was called into Mrs. Freedman's office. I was relieved to see that she already had my resumé on her desk. After some small talk, Mrs. Freedman asked me about my experience in the Financial Club at school. I gave her more details about the club and the other activities I listed on my resumé. She asked some questions about my plans for the future and even suggested a good economics professor at Brown!

When it was time for me to ask questions about the job, I asked about the day-to-day responsibilities. Mrs. Freedman said that she was looking for someone who could file, keep track of accounts, and talk to clients and answer their questions. Mrs. Freedman would supervise the work, but the job was largely the responsibility of the person she was hiring. I told her I was excited about the possibility of learning so much at a summer job. I said it sounded challenging, but I was ready to do whatever was necessary to get it done!"

Luckily, Alicia's early mistakes did not hurt her interview. A ringing cell phone could have cost her the job. Inspite of the cell phone and not being prepared with extra copies of her resumé, Alicia had a

Make eye contact and sit up straight. Your interviewer will be impressed if you present yourself well.

Smile, relax, and be yourself—the interview is your time to shine.

very successful interview. She had confirmed her appointment the day before and she arrived early for the interview. She dressed conservatively and filled in the details when she was talking about her work experience. She also expressed her interest in doing something challenging and being willing to make sure it got done correctly. Even if Alicia wasn't hired for the job, she had every reason to feel good about her job interview.

Having a good attitude will make any interview more enjoyable—and more successful.

Chapter 4

A World of Possibilities

Don't forget to think about other kinds of jobs in your search. Volunteer work is unpaid, but volunteering looks great on your resumé and school records. Volunteer work is usually done for charities or other organizations like parks, churches, schools, or health agencies.

As a student, you may be able to work as an intern. An internship is usually a job for a student to gain experience and learn about a certain field. An internship can take many forms, and can be paid or unpaid. You could intern at a magazine, or work as a research assistant at a university. Check with your guidance counselor or with a company that you are interested in to get details about internships.

Most help-wanted ads are usually printed in newspapers on the weekends. This can be a great resource for job openings.

Persistence Pays Off

Even qualified people who have terrific job interviews don't always get the job they want. It can be discouraging to learn that you've been turned down for a job. If you are, don't get frustrated. Finding a job requires special skills. As you learn these skills, allow yourself some setbacks. Remember when you first learned how to ride a bike, play a game, or play an instrument? It took time to learn how to do these things well. It's the same with job hunting. It will take time to learn the skills to find a good job. But remember, the better your job-hunting skills become, the better your chances of getting your dream job. Good luck!

> Be sure to check job postings often, you never know when a new opportunity will arise.

New Words

advertisement a public notice

confirm to make sure that something is true or is definitely happening

conservative moderate, cautious, not extreme

employer a person who hires others to work for him or her

intern someone who is learning a skill or job by working with an expert in the field

interview a meeting in which an employer speaks with an applicant

networking talking to people about jobs and careers

New Words

resumé a brief list of the jobs, education, and awards a person has had

transferable skills skills that are not job-related

volunteer someone who works without being paid

For Further Reading

Anselmi, John. *The Yale Daily News Guide to Internships 2000*. New York, NY: Simon & Schuster Trade, 2000.

Culbreath, Alice N. *Testing the Waters: A Teen's Guide to Career Exploration*. Lewes, DE: JRC Consulting, 1999.

Fry, Ron. *Your First Resume: For Students and Anyone Preparing to Enter Today's Tough Job Market*. Franklin Lakes, NJ: Career Press, 2001.

Marques, Eva. *100 Jobs for Kids & Young Adults— A Self-Empowerment Tool*. Chicago, IL: WiseChild Press, 1997.

Organizations
The Princeton Review
2315 Broadway
New York, NY 10024
(212) 874-8282
www.review.com

U. S. Department of Labor
200 Constitution Avenue, NW
Washington, DC 20210
(866) 4-USA-DOL
www.dol.gov

Web Sites
QuintCareers: Teenage Jobs, Careers, and College
www.quintcareers.com
This Web site has a lot of information about finding jobs and making decisions about college and your career. It is made just for teenagers.

SnagAJob.com
www.snagajob.com
This Web site has many kinds of jobs for you to apply for. Many different companies advertise on this unique Web site.

Studentjobs.gov
www.studentjobs.gov
This Web site has a lot of government jobs for students.

SummerJobs.com
www.summerjobs.com
Use this Web site to find a great summer job.